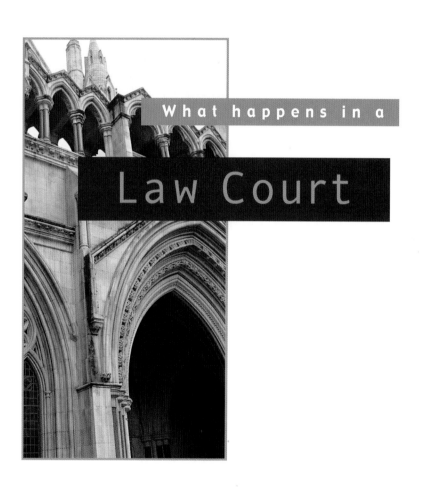

What happens in a

Law Court

Citizen Guides

What happens in a

Law Court

How the courts work

Dan Lambeth

W

FRANKLIN WATTS
LONDON•SYDNEY

About the author

Dan Lambeth studied law at the University of Oxford before training as a solicitor at the London law firm Clifford Chance. He now works at the Law Society where he advises on civil justice and the courts.

Note

The information in this book is provided as a guide only. No responsibility is accepted by or on behalf of the publisher or the author for any errors, omissions or misleading statements.

Key words

To help you find your way around this book, key words are printed in **bold**. You can find some of these words in the glossary on pages 30-31.

Illustrations Alastair Taylor/The Inkshed

Designer Magda Weldon
Editor Penny Clarke
Art Director Jonathan Hair
Editor-in-Chief John C. Miles

© 2000 Franklin Watts

First published in 2000
by Franklin Watts
96 Leonard Street
London
EC2A 4XD

Franklin Watts Australia
14 Mars Road
Lane Cove
NSW 2066

ISBN 0 7496 3762 5

Dewey classification: 347

A CIP catalogue record
for this book is available
from the British Library.

Printed in Malaysia

Contents

This book aims to explain the role that the law and the courts have in our lives. It looks at the history of the courts, the role of judges and lawyers and uses two case studies to illustrate civil and criminal cases.

What the courts do

The **law** and the **courts** help people to solve problems. Law courts deal with two main types of problem: **civil** and **criminal**.

Civil cases are mainly **disputes** between private individuals. When married couples divorce, there may be arguments about how to divide property such as a house. The court might order that the matrimonial home should be sold and the proceeds evenly divided. Another example might be a business dispute involving a **debt** or some

THE HIGH COURT in London is the centre of the English court system.

substandard work. In such a case the court might decide that one business should pay money (called **damages**) to another business to repay the debt or as **compensation** for the poor work.

Criminal cases are disputes that involve the state – the **police** and the **Crown Prosecution Service (CPS)**. Crimes include physical **assault** and harassment, **damage** to property and **theft**. For these **offences** the courts can impose **fines** and, in serious cases, order **imprisonment**.

Politicians and judges

Both politicians and **judges** possess a great deal of power. However, their roles are quite different and there are clear rules about if and to what extent they can interfere in each other's work.

Put simply, politicians make laws; judges are responsible for applying them. However, it is not possible for politicians to pass laws that cover every type of problem. In these cases, judges can make the law, but Parliament can change it later.

Judges can also question whether a law was properly made by Parliament, or whether a politician has made a wrong decision.

The English legal system

The system of law used in England and Wales is known as **common law**. It is possible to trace this back to very old English customs. Other countries, such as the United States, Canada and Australia also use common law systems.

Common law is based partly on the decisions of judges. These decisions must normally be followed by other judges. This is known as **precedent**.

The courts

The **courts** of England and Wales have grown from the royal 'courts' of kings and queens. The old royal courts were not courts in the modern sense. They were the places where the **monarch** and his or her **advisers** lived and made decisions about important questions.

However, the right of the monarch to control all his or her country's affairs was steadily challenged until deciding cases of **law** became the sole job of **judges**.

The early legal system

Before the **Norman Conquest** in 1066 there was no one system of law or courts in England. Cases were dealt with by the unwritten **customs** of the particular area in which the problem arose. These **local customs** were the habitual or usual way of doing things. Cases were not decided by professional judges and there were no written rules on how to deal with specific problems.

The system of law and courts as we know them today grew out of the **Norman conquest** of England in 1066. The Normans liked organisation and helped develop a single system of courts. This in turn brought more unity and consistency to the law.

The Normans under William I's rule were particularly concerned to build a good **criminal legal system** to ensure peace and order throughout the kingdom. In addition, the **fines** paid by criminals helped to boost the king's finances.

ORIGINALLY, a 'court' was where the monarch lived with his or her advisers.

At first, legal decisions were made at the King's Court, which moved from place to place.

Development and reform

Originally the **King's Court,** or the Court of **King's** or **Queen's Bench,** the name by which it is still known, dealt mainly with the monarch's affairs. It also had control over **criminal cases,** as widespread crime could threaten the stability of the kingdom. Over time, however, this court lost its links with the king or queen.

A second court, called the **Court of Common Pleas,** developed around 1230. This court dealt with cases that did not directly involve the king.

The third court to develop was the **Exchequer.** Originally the king used the Exchequer to collect money owed to him. The Exchequer became so good at this that ordinary people began to use it in money cases.

By the eighteenth century, the powers of these three courts were fairly equal. However, some courts got more work than others. So in 1875 it was decided to create one single **High Court,** which still exists.

Scotland

Scotland has a separate system of courts and law from England and Wales. When the two kingdoms were united in 1707 it was decided that while there should be only one Parliament, Scotland should retain its separate legal system and courts.

Scottish law developed very differently from English law. Historically, it is closer to the law of the ancient Romans than English law. The most important Scottish courts are the **Court of Session** and the **High Court of Justiciary.** Scottish lawyers are known as **advocates** and **solicitors.**

There are several types of court. Some courts specialise in civil cases; others in criminal cases. Local courts deal with everyday cases, while the High Court and appeal courts deal with high-profile ones.

Civil cases

Civil cases are heard by the High Court, county courts and magistrates' courts. The **High Court** is one of the most important courts in England and Wales. It deals with more complex and high-value civil cases.

The High Court is made up of several departments, or **divisions**, including the **Queen's Bench**, **Chancery** and **Family** Divisions.

Each division specialises in certain types of case and although based in London they also travel around the country.

For example, the Chancery Division deals with, among other things, trade and business disputes. It is based at the High Court in London but also handles cases in other cities.

House of Lords

Court of Appeal

The High Court

Crown court

County court

Magistrates' court

Magistrates' court

CRIMINAL CASES

CIVIL CASES

THIS SIMPLIFIED DIAGRAM shows how courts are ranked. Less serious cases are handled by lower courts; the appeal courts are at the top.

County courts deal with less serious civil cases. They handle disputes about money, some **divorce** and **family** cases, **personal injury** (for example, if you slip and hurt yourself on the pavement), **contracts** and **housing repossession**.

Magistrates' courts, the third type of court dealing with civil cases, are concerned mainly with cases of **debt**, such as non-payment of taxes.

Criminal cases

Criminal cases are heard by either the **Crown court** or the **Magistrates' court**. Crown courts handle the more serious criminal cases. Unlike most civil cases, which are only decided by judges, criminal cases in the Crown court are decided by a **judge** and a **jury** (up to 12 ordinary members of the public who listen to the facts presented and decide if the accused is guilty or innocent).

Magistrates' courts deal with the less serious criminal cases such as **traffic offences**. Many cases are heard by **lay magistrates**. Lay magistrates, sometimes known as **Justices of the Peace** or **JPs**, are unpaid ordinary members of the public who hear cases about once every fortnight.

There are also **stipendiary magistrates** who are paid and work full-time.

Appeals

People can **appeal** when they are unhappy with the decision of a lower court. Appeals are heard by the **High Court,** the **Court of Appeal** and the **House of Lords.**

All these courts deal with civil and criminal cases. They study the facts of the case and can overrule the decision of a lower court. In some cases, they may order a re-trial.

The **House of Lords** is unusual in that it is both the Upper House of Parliament and also the highest court of appeal.

People who are unhappy with the decision of a court may complain or 'appeal' to a higher court.

Judges decide the cases presented to them in court. The most senior judges are appointed by the Queen on the advice of the Prime Minister in consultation with the Lord Chancellor.

Making decisions

Judges **adjudicate** or **try** cases, that is they help to solve problems or arguments. To do this the judge listens to both sides of an argument. To reach a **decision** he or she examines the law and applies it to the facts of the particular case. The judge gives reasons for reaching the decision. The decision and its reasoning will often be published in books called **law reports**. Law reports act as a guide to the law for other judges, lawyers and members of the public.

In criminal cases in the **Crown court**, judges work with a jury. After the lawyers for each side have given their version of the case, the judge **sums up** the **evidence** and gives the jury advice on the law. It is then left to the jury to decide whether the defendant is **guilty** or **innocent**. The judge then decides the appropriate **sentence** for the **offence** that has been committed.

Senior judges

The most senior judges in England and Wales are the **Lord Chancellor**, the **Lord Chief Justice**, the **Master of the Rolls** and the **Vice-Chancellor**. The Lord Chancellor, as head of the **judiciary**, is the most senior. Although rarely sitting as a judge, he has the right to decide cases in the **House of Lords**.

IN EARLIER TIMES, judges worked directly for the king or queen. If the monarch did not like a decision, the judge could be sacked.

JUDGES 'PROCESS' in London to mark the start of the new legal year.

Judges normally work alone, but in high-profile cases they may work in groups.

Appointing judges

Being a judge is an important job. In Britain, lawyers with many years' experience may apply to become judges. In most cases, it is the Lord Chancellor who decides who can become a judge.

In other countries, especially those that have **civil law systems**, it is not necessary to be a lawyer to become a judge. People can become judges by undertaking a period of training.

Independence

Today, judges are independent and cannot be sacked if the Crown or the government do not like a decision. This means that judges can concentrate solely on cases without having to worry about outside factors.

Solicitors and barristers

The history of lawyers in England and Wales dates back to the 1200s, when advisers called attorneys assisted the king. Today there are two main types of lawyers – solicitors and barristers.

Solicitors

Solicitors first appeared in the fifteenth century. They got this name because they 'solicited' causes. This means that they gave advice and appointed **barristers**. When people have legal problems, they see a solicitor first.

Solicitors, whose offices can be found on most local High Streets, do many different types of work. They give people legal advice and help them to buy and sell houses and to write **wills**. If someone wants to **go to court**, solicitors can advise on whether there is a good case. If the case does go to court, the solicitor assembles all the important papers. This is called the **brief**. It is sent to the barrister so that he or she has all the facts about the case.

THE LAW SOCIETY regulates the work of solicitors in England and Wales.

Barristers

Another name for a **barrister** is **counsel**. The work of the barrister normally begins when he or she receives a **brief** from a **solicitor**. The barrister will often give an opinion as to whether the **client** has a good case. If the case **goes to court** it is normally the barrister who **represents** the client – he or she speaks to the judge in court on behalf of the client. Sometimes, however, the solicitor will be able to speak to the judge.

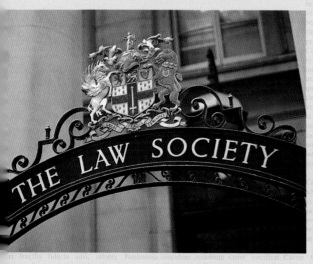

A BARRISTER – dressed in traditional wig and gown – advises a client.

Representing someone in court is called **advocacy**. Advocacy involves explaining the problem and asking for a solution. After listening to the lawyers for each side, the judge makes a decision and orders a solution.

Regulating the professions

Anyone who wants to become a solicitor or a barrister must pass exams and do appropriate work experience. The **Law Society** and the **General Council of the Bar** are the professional organisations responsible for making sure that law students have fulfilled the necessary requirements. They also set rules for solicitors and barristers.

Scotland

In Scotland lawyers are known as **solicitors** and **advocates**. They do work similar to English solicitors and barristers. They are represented by the **Law Society of Scotland** and the **Faculty of Advocates**.

As well as judges and lawyers, other professionals play important roles in the legal system. These include the police, the Crown Prosecution Service (CPS), the probation service and voluntary organisations.

POLICE help to prevent crime by keeping a high profile. Here, two constables patrol an airport terminal.

The police

The **police service** is split into divisions serving different regions of Britain. Police help to prevent **crime** and to **keep the peace** in various ways, for example by patrolling the streets. Unfortunately, the police are unable to prevent all crime.

When a crime is reported, the police undertake an **investigation**. They may detain, question and charge **suspects**. Being **charged** with a crime means being officially accused of it. The papers accusing the person of the crime will then be sent to the **Crown Prosecution Service (CPS)**.

The Crown Prosecution Service

The **Crown Prosecution Service** is a government department. It acts as the lawyer for the **victim** of a crime and decides whether the person accused of the crime should go to court. This is called deciding whether to **'prosecute'** somebody. In court, the victim of the crime is represented by a barrister appointed by the CPS.

The probation service

It can be difficult to decide how to punish criminals. **Probation officers** help judges to learn more about the character of the criminals that appear before them. With the help of probation officers, the judge will be able to decide, for example, whether someone should go to **prison**, or whether it would be better to punish them in a different way. Probation officers also help offenders to get used to life after prison.

Supporting victims of crime

Being the victim of a crime can be a very upsetting experience. The organisation **Victim Support** helps people to deal with the experience of being a victim of crime. Volunteers working for Victim Support may visit the victim to help them talk about their feelings and to offer support.

Citizens' Advice Bureaux

Solicitors' and barristers' fees can be very high. **Citizens' Advice Bureaux (CAB)** and some other advice agencies are able to provide people with free legal advice. However, staff at advice agencies are not always legally qualified and it may be necessary also to consult a lawyer.

The two fictional case studies that follow will help to show how the court system of England and Wales works on a day-to-day basis and demonstrate some basic differences between civil and criminal cases.

Darren Green's shopping trip

Darren Green is 26 years old. One Saturday, Darren goes to the supermarket. On the way, he trips on a cracked pavement and falls. The injury is bad enough for him to have to go to hospital. At the A & E Department the doctor tells Darren that he has broken his ankle. Darren is very angry.

Starting a civil claim

Darren sees a **solicitor** about the accident. He explains that he believes that the accident was the **fault** of the council for failing to repair the cracked pavement.

The solicitor writes to the council to complain about the accident and to ask for money to be paid to Darren to **compensate** him. The money is meant to make up for the pain and annoyance Darren has experienced.

The council, however, refuses to pay Darren any money, arguing that the accident was his fault because he wasn't looking where he was going.

Darren and the solicitor decide to go to court to resolve the problem. Details of the accident are written down on a **claim form** which is sent to the court.

Unlike criminal cases, the police are normally not involved in a civil case.

3 Evidence

5 Compensation

1 Accident

4 Trial

2 Solicitor

A CIVIL CASE

Evidence

To prove the case, Darren and his solicitor must provide **evidence** to help the judge decide the case in court. It might be **photographs**, **interviews** or a **report** by an **expert witness**. In this case, Darren's solicitor arranges for photographs to be taken of the cracked pavement. The solicitor also interviews a passer-by who saw the accident. All this evidence is sent to the court.

The trial

At the **trial** Darren is represented by a **barrister**. The council also has its own barrister. Each barrister explains their client's side of the story to the judge.

After listening to the barristers and seeing the evidence, the judge decides that the accident was the fault of the council and orders it to pay Darren **damages** – a sum of money to **compensate** him for the accident. The judge also orders the council to pay the fees of Darren's barrister and solicitor. This is known as **costs**.

In the civil case, Darren Green was able to make his own decisions about whether to go to court. In criminal cases, the Crown Prosecution Service (CPS) decides whether or not the case should go to court.

The CPS decides whether or not there is enough evidence for a criminal case to go to court.

Sue Palmer's unwelcome visitor

Sue Palmer returns home after work one afternoon to discover that her flat has been burgled. The police are called. They question Sue and talk to neighbours. Someone reports having seen a stranger leave Sue's flat that day.

The police and the CPS

Thanks to the neighbour's description of the burglar, the police **arrest** and **charge** a man named Tony Stevens with the burglary.

Tony denies the charge. He is not detained at the station but is released on **bail** – he is free to go but must appear in court later. The police send the **case papers** to the CPS, who decide that there is enough **evidence** for a **court case**.

Magistrates' court or Crown court?

Burglary is an **either-way offence** – the case can be heard either in a **Magistrates' court** or in a **Crown court**. The main difference is that Crown court cases are dealt with by juries as well as by a judge.

At a **mode of trial hearing** before magistrates, Tony decides to ask the Crown court to hear his case. He believes that his case will be dealt with more

2 Arrest

4 Punishment

1 Crime

3 Trial – either at Magistrates' court or Crown court

A CRIMINAL CASE

carefully if a jury is present. The CPS does not object and the magistrates agree.

As in civil cases, Sue and Tony have their own barristers. Sue's barrister is appointed by the CPS. Before the trial, each barrister receives a brief from the solicitors. At the trial, Tony gives his side of the story. This is listened to by the judge and the jury. The jury decides that Tony is guilty of the burglary.

Sentencing

After the trial, the judge decides on the correct **sentence**. The **Probation Service** prepares a **pre-sentence report**. The report helps the judge to decide on the best way of punishing Tony for the crime. Tony's barrister makes a **plea in mitigation**. This is a request for a lighter punishment. The barrister tells the court that as Tony is only 18 years old and was pressured into committing the crime, he should only receive a light sentence. However, because Tony has committed burglary before, he is sentenced to serve six months in a **Young Offenders' Institution**.

Various remedies and punishments are available to the courts in both civil and criminal cases. Prison is the obvious criminal punishment, but less drastic solutions may be better in the long run.

The courts have many remedies and punishments available to them.

Civil remedies

Darren took the council to court because of his fall on the pavement. The courts can offer many different types of solution in civil cases.

Money

The courts can order people to pay money. This can happen, for example, when money is owed.

In Darren's case money had to be paid to **compensate** him for pain and inconvenience.

Action

In some cases the court may order a **party** to do something which he or she had promised to do in a **contract**, but had subsequently failed or refused to do.

The courts will not order this remedy if it means that it has to supervise **compliance** or if it involves personal work or service.

Apology

The courts can make people **apologise** if they have made false written or spoken statements that make another person look bad to other people. This area of law is called **defamation**. If an untrue statement is written down, it is known as **libel**; if spoken it is **slander**.

Money – compensation or fine

Imprisonment

Apology

Community service

SOME OF THE MANY forms of civil remedy and criminal punishment.

In earlier times there were many terrible forms of punishment, which included branding with a hot iron, hanging and being pressed to death with weights. Today, the law employs much more humane ways of punishing criminals.

Prison

The traditional punishment for crime is **imprisonment**. The length of **sentence** varies – the more serious a crime, the more time the criminal is likely to spend in prison.

Fines

Sometimes, people who commit crimes are compelled to pay money **fines**.

Community work

Instead of prison a criminal may be made to serve a **community sentence** for a specific number of hours. This may include a **community service order**.

A community service order requires the criminal to participate in a community project. For example, it may involve clearing derelict land or painting an old building.

Probation

There are ways that the court can keep an eye on criminals without sending them to prison. One way is to require the criminal to visit a **probation officer** regularly. The officer will try to help the criminal not to commit any more offences, thus protecting the public from further harm.

Another way is for the offender to agree not to leave his or her home between certain hours – this is called a **curfew**. The criminal may be fitted with an **electronic tag** to make sure he or she complies.

Going to court can be very expensive. Lawyers charge hourly fees for their services, and courts charge for their use. If, however, you are unable to afford these costs, you may still be able to go to court.

Solicitors and barristers

There are many ways that solicitors and barristers can be paid. They can be paid up front, as the case progresses, or after the case is over. You may agree to pay according to the outcome of the case. This is called a **conditional fee arrangement**. Some solicitors also give free first interviews.

In some cases lawyers will work for free. This type of work is called **pro bono**. One form of pro bono work is the provision of free legal advice in advice centres.

LEGAL AID is available to those on low incomes or with little savings.

Legal aid

If people are unable to afford the cost of going to court, the **Legal Aid Board** may be able to help. The Legal Aid Board will shortly change its name to the **Legal Services Commission**.

This organisation helps people with some or all of the cost of going to court. The solicitor takes into account a client's **savings** and **earnings** to work out whether he or she is eligible for legal aid. Not all solicitors provide this type of help.

Legal aid is only available for the following categories of case: divorce, family problems, criminal cases, debt cases, problems possibly caused by hospitals and doctors, and rent and mortgage cases.

When deciding whether someone can get legal aid the Board also looks at savings and earnings. In **civil cases**, the Board will assess the chances of the case succeeding. If the case is won, the **claimant** may be asked to use the money or property awarded by the court to pay the bill.

Questioned by police?

Everyone is entitled to free legal advice if they are **questioned by the police**, irrespective of their earnings and savings. At the police station suspects are given an information sheet telling them about their rights and they will be advised either by the **duty solicitor** (an independent lawyer not employed by the police) or a solicitor of their choice.

People are also entitled to free legal advice and possibly free representation at a **Magistrates' court**. However, most people arrange for advice and representation before attending court.

There are many ways to pay for the cost of going to court.

Although judges are independent, the government is responsible for running the courts. The two government departments involved are the Lord Chancellor's Department and the Home Office.

THE LORD CHANCELLOR is a member of the government. Here he is at the State Opening of Parliament.

The Lord Chancellor's Department

The **Lord Chancellor's Department (LCD)** is responsible for making sure that the law and courts work well. This involves appointing judges, supervising the courts, handling legal aid and arranging changes to the law.

The LCD is responsible for most of the courts, except for Magistrates' courts. These are the responsibility of local councils. The LCD is assisted in its work by the **Court Service** which is an **executive agency** of the government. It deals with administrative and operational matters.

The Home Office

The **Home Office** is responsible for ensuring law and order in the country. In particular it looks at ways of reducing crime and improving the justice system. It has responsibility for the police, prison and probation services and also for **immigration policy** – deciding who can and cannot enter the country.

Although the **Home Secretary** is a member of the **government**, he or she does occasionally engage in judicial decision-making. For example, he or she is responsible for deciding **extradition orders**, when a person is sent to another country to face trial.

English judges must follow EU law. If there is a conflict, European law must be followed

The European Union

The **European Union (EU)**, established in 1951, is made up of 15 European countries – including Britain, which joined in 1973. The countries of the EU try to work together on issues such as farming and the economy. In order to work efficiently it is important to have rules to settle difficult and important issues. Therefore, the EU has its own law and courts.

European law is made up of **treaties**, **regulations**, **directives** and the **decisions** of the European courts. The most important court, founded in 1952, is the **European Court of Justice**.

In cases where European law is unclear, English courts can refer the issue to the European courts. If countries or companies break European law, they may be forced to pay large fines.

THE EUROPEAN COURT OF JUSTICE is situated in Luxembourg.

United States of America

The law of the United States of America is historically based on the English **common law** system. However, today the USA's legal system differs from the English system in many ways.

The USA has a **dual legal system** – two sets of laws and courts. The whole country shares a set of laws called **federal law**. However, each **state** is entitled to develop its own laws as long as they do not conflict with federal law.

The USA has a written **constitution** which guarantees US citizens certain **rights**, such as free speech. The courts interpret these rights.

In the USA there is no distinction between solicitors and barristers. However, it is possible, for example, to specialise in **advocacy**. Each state has its own rules regulating lawyers. A lawyer qualified to **practise** in the state of California would be unable to practise in the state of New York without passing the local legal examinations.

The highest court in the USA is the **Supreme Court**. Judges are appointed to the Supreme Court by the **President**.

Australia

Australia has a common law system, like Britain. It is divided into states like the USA, and it has a written constitution. Each state is entitled to develop its own laws but, as in the USA, these

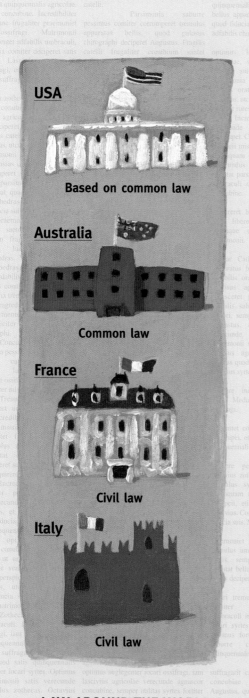

USA

Based on common law

Australia

Common law

France

Civil law

Italy

Civil law

LAW AROUND THE WORLD

must not conflict with federal law. The legal profession is regulated at state level.

The Queen is **Head of State** in Australia and exercises her power through the **Attorney-General**. English and Australian law share many similarities. The **High Court of Australia** is responsible for interpreting the **constitution** and hears **appeals** from **state courts**.

 France

France has a **civil law** system. French law is based on collections of laws called **codes**, together with **ordinances**, **decrees** and **statutes**. As in England, French judges play some role in interpreting the law. However, their decisions are not binding. Also, more attention is paid to the writings of **law teachers** – but again, these are not binding.

The supreme courts are called the **Conseil d'Etat** and the **Cour de Cassation**. There are 28 Courts of Appeal. The **Tribunaux de Grande Instance** deal with civil cases and **Courts of Assize** and **Correctional Courts** with criminal cases. French lawyers are known as **avocats**.

 Italy

Like France, Italy has a civil law system based on a series of **codes**. The law is also made up of the **constitution**, **statutes** and **regulations**. Italian courts are headed by the **Corte Suprema di Cassazione**.

Judges do not come from the legal profession, they are **civil servants** who train to become judges. A lawyer begins working life as an attorney or **procuratore legale** and after some time may become an **avvocato**.

Barrister — Lawyer specialising in advocacy.

Civil law — Law dealing with disputes between citizens.

Civil legal system — Legal system based partly on codes, which places less reliance than the common law system on precedents and the decisions of judges.

Claimant — Party starting a civil claim.

Common law system — Legal system based partly on the decisions of judges, with reliance on precedent.

County court — Court that deals with minor civil claims.

Court of Appeal — Court that hears appeals from lower courts.

Court of Session — A Scottish court.

Court Service — Government agency dealing with the administration of the courts.

Criminal law — Law dealing with disputes that disrupt peace and order and involve the police.

Crown Prosecution Service — Government agency that represents victims of crime in court.

Damages — Money paid as compensation in civil claims.

Defendant — The person accused in a court of law.

Either-way offence — Criminal offence that may be tried in either a Magistrates' court or a Crown court.

European Court of Justice	Court that deals with European law.
General Council of the Bar	The professional body that regulates and supports barristers.
House of Lords	The highest court of appeal in the UK.
Judge	The official who decides cases in court.
Jury	Group of 12 members of the public who decide if a defendant is guilty or innocent in criminal cases.
Law Society	The professional body that regulates and supports solicitors.
Lay magistrate	Unpaid member of the public who acts as a judge in the Magistrates' court.
Legal Aid Board	Government agency that pays for legal advice and representation.
Lord Chancellor	The member of the government who is also the head of the judiciary in England and Wales.
Magistrates' court	Court that deals with minor civil and criminal cases.
Precedent	System in which judges follow decisions made by other judges.
Probation service	Government agency that provides judges with information about convicted offenders and assists offenders when they leave prison.
Solicitor	Lawyer.
Stipendiary magistrate	A paid judge in the Magistrates' court.
Trial	Hearing at which a case is decided by a judge.